MW01537424

This notebook belongs to:

____

Published by Neaterstuff Publishing

Made in the USA
Las Vegas, NV
13 May 2022

48831346R00069